Fire and Ash

Written by Mary Atkinson

Costa Rica

My name is Imelda. I live in Costa Rica. There are lots of volcanoes in my country. Do you know what a volcano is? What do you think causes a volcano?

Contents

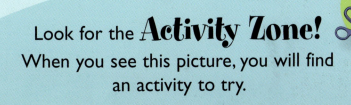

Look for the **Activity Zone!**
When you see this picture, you will find
an activity to try.

Volcano Country

Costa Rica has about 112 volcanoes. Some are *active*. Lava, huge rocks, and deadly gases pour out of them. Some are not active at the moment. They are *dormant*. Others will probably never be active again. We say they are *extinct*.

The volcanoes in Costa Rica form a chain of mountains down the middle of the country. Most people live on high ground up in the mountains. There it is cool, and plants grow well.

Arenal has been an active volcano since 1968. Before that, it was a dormant volcano for 400 years.

lava   hot, melted rock that has come out of the ground

The air on a volcanic mountain can smell like rotten eggs. This is caused by sulfur, a mineral often found around volcanoes.

This map shows six major volcanoes in Costa Rica. Irazú is the highest, and Arenal is the most active.

Caribbean Sea

▲ Rincón de la Vieja

▲ Arenal
Miravalles ▲

▲ Poás

Turrialba
San José ⭐ ▲▲ Irazú

COSTA RICA

NORTH PACIFIC OCEAN

The Ring of Fire

Costa Rica lies on the Ring of Fire.
This is a circle of countries around
the Pacific Ocean that all have volcanoes.

Most scientists think the earth's outside crust
is broken into several pieces, called *plates*.
The plates move very slowly—just a few inches
a year. However, when two plates push against
each other, this can cause volcanoes
and earthquakes. The Ring of Fire
is where several plates meet.

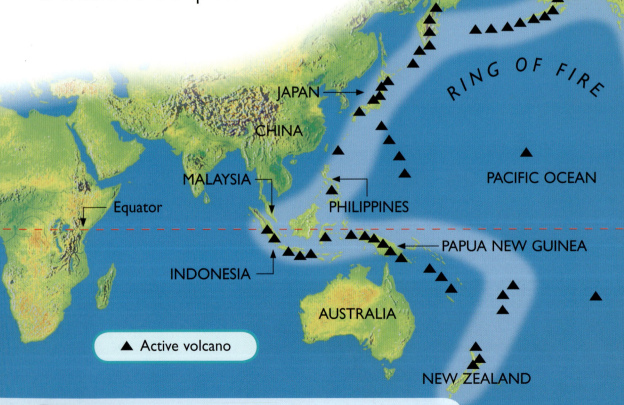

RUSSIA

RING OF FIRE

JAPAN →

CHINA

MALAYSIA

PACIFIC OCEAN

PHILIPPINES

Equator

PAPUA NEW GUINEA

INDONESIA

AUSTRALIA

▲ Active volcano

NEW ZEALAND

earthquake when the ground moves or shakes

6

At night, the red-hot lava thrown out of Arenal lights up the dark sky.

Around the Ring

1. In 1943, a Mexican farmer saw a crack appear in his cornfield. It was the beginning of the Paricutin volcano, which was active until 1952.

2. Mount Fuji is Japan's highest mountain. It is a dormant volcano. It was last active in 1708.

3. Mount Ruapehu is an active volcano in New Zealand. People were skiing on the mountain the last time it erupted. They got off the mountain quickly, and no one was hurt.

NORTH AMERICA

COSTA RICA

SOUTH AMERICA

1

2

3

Eruption!

An eruption is an explosion of lava, rocks, gas, and ash. It begins when rock melts into magma deep inside the earth. Magma is full of gases. It rises up through cracks in the earth's crust and then bursts onto the surface as a volcano.

When the lava cools, it becomes solid rock. It often builds up around a volcano, creating a new mountain.

magma   hot, melted rock inside the earth

This diagram shows what happens when there is an eruption.

1. Ash
2. Rocks
3. Lava
4. Rock formed from cooled lava
5. Magma

Mount St. Helens in Washington state erupted on May 18, 1980. One whole side of the mountain was blown away.

Inside a Volcano

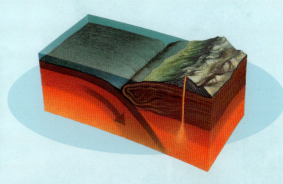

When an ocean plate meets a land plate, the thinner ocean plate is pushed under the land. It melts into magma and then rises up, creating a volcano. The Ring of Fire volcanoes were formed in this way.

When two ocean plates meet, one is pushed under the other. This causes volcanoes that create islands in the sea. The Hawaiian islands formed this way.

Lava Flows

Different types of lava cause different types of volcanoes. In Costa Rica, thick, sticky lava explodes out of the ground in violent eruptions. Rock and ash are thrown high into the air.

Runny lava causes less violent eruptions. In Hawaii, runny lava flows quickly down mountain slopes, covering the land below. It can travel up to 100 miles before cooling into rock.

violent   having great force that can cause harm

Costa Rica's volcanoes have sticky lava. Rocks explode out of the mountains.

Runny lava from Kilauea volcano, in Hawaii, flows into the sea. The cold water cools the lava quickly, giving off lots of steam.

From Lava to Rock

Pumice

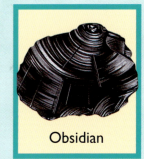

Obsidian

- Pumice forms from bubbly, gas-filled lava. This rock has so many bubbles that it floats!

- Obsidian is a natural glass. It forms from smooth lava that cools quickly. Obsidian is so sharp that the ancient Aztecs used it to make blades.

Basalt

Rhyolite

- Basalt and rhyolite are other rocks that form from cooled lava.

Ash, Dust, and Bombs

Many volcanoes throw rocks high into the air. The tiniest pieces of rock are so small that they are called *volcanic dust*. They float up into the atmosphere. Slightly bigger pieces are called *volcanic ash*. Piles of hot ash cool into solid rock.

The biggest rocks are called *volcanic bombs*. They can be the size of a pebble or the size of a truck. These rocks can cause a lot of damage.

atmosphere the layers of air and gas surrounding the earth

This large boulder is actually a volcanic bomb that was blown out of a volcano.

When Quito, in Ecuador, erupted in 2002, thick clouds of ash fell on city streets. The ash made it hard to breathe.

Ash in the Wind

Wind direction

A powerful volcano can shoot clouds of ash and dust high into the sky. At about 12 miles high, the cloud reaches strong winds that carry it around the world.

Volcanic ash in the atmosphere can cause cold weather. It can also cause colorful sunsets around the world.

13

Rivers of Mud and Gas

When volcanic ash mixes with river water or rainwater, it turns into mud. Mudflows can cause floods that wipe out farms and towns.

Sometimes a mix of hot gas, ash, and rock flows down the side of a volcano. It can travel faster than 100 miles an hour. The poisonous gases are deadly, and they are hot enough to melt metal.

In 1991, a flow of gas, ash, and rock from Mt. Unzen in southern Japan wiped out 705 homes. Nearly 9,000 people were evacuated.

evacuate to leave a dangerous place

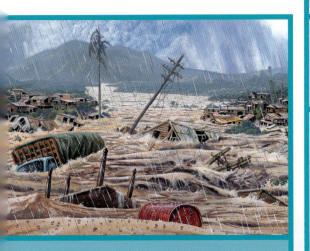

Years after a volcano, heavy rain can mix with volcanic ash to create mudflows, called *lahars*.

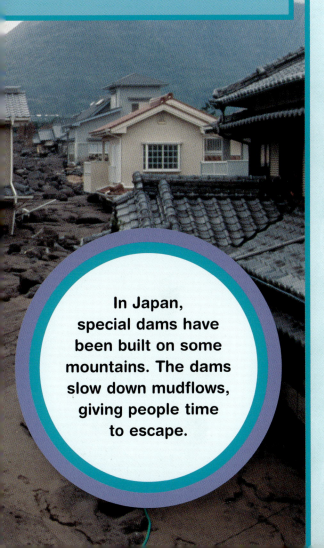

In Japan, special dams have been built on some mountains. The dams slow down mudflows, giving people time to escape.

The Buried Town

In A.D. 79, Mount Vesuvius in Italy erupted. The nearby town of Pompeii was covered by a flow of gas and ash. Archaeologists have dug out the old town, and now people can visit it.

archaeologist a scientist who studies things left by ancient societies

Craters and Lakes

When a volcano stops erupting, it leaves
a huge hole at the top of the mountain.
This hole is called a *crater*. It is the place where
the lava, gas, and rock came out. Any mountain
that has a crater was once an active volcano.

Craters often fill up with rainwater. They become
crater lakes. If a small amount of hot gas is still
coming out of the mountain, the lake heats up.

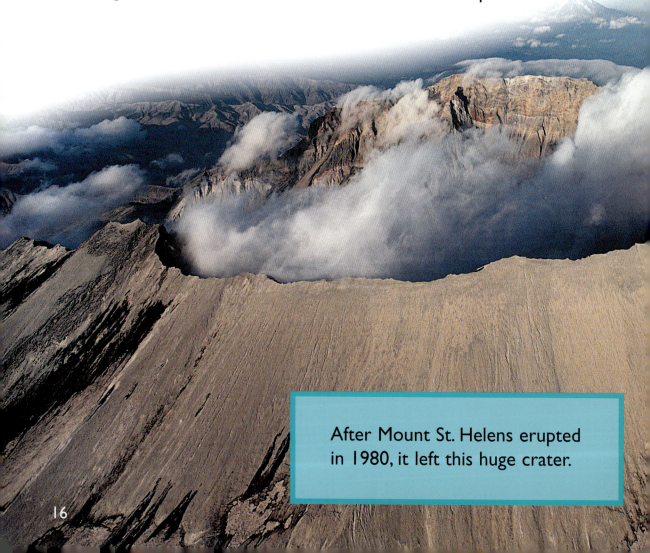

After Mount St. Helens erupted
in 1980, it left this huge crater.

The deepest lake in the United States is called *Crater Lake*. It is 1,932 feet deep and is at the top of Mount Mazama, a dormant volcano.

After the Eruption

Poás volcano in Costa Rica has the second biggest crater in the world. It is nearly 5,000 feet wide. The water in its crater lake is boiling hot.

This old crater is on an extinct volcano. It is now part of a park in the middle of Auckland city in New Zealand.

Studying Volcanoes

Some scientists study volcanoes. They are called *volcanologists*. They find out new things about the rocks inside the earth. They also help figure out when a volcano will erupt next. This can save thousands of lives.

Volcanologists have an unsafe job. When they go near active volcanoes, they have to wear plenty of safety gear. Where possible, they use planes or satellites to find out what is happening inside a volcano.

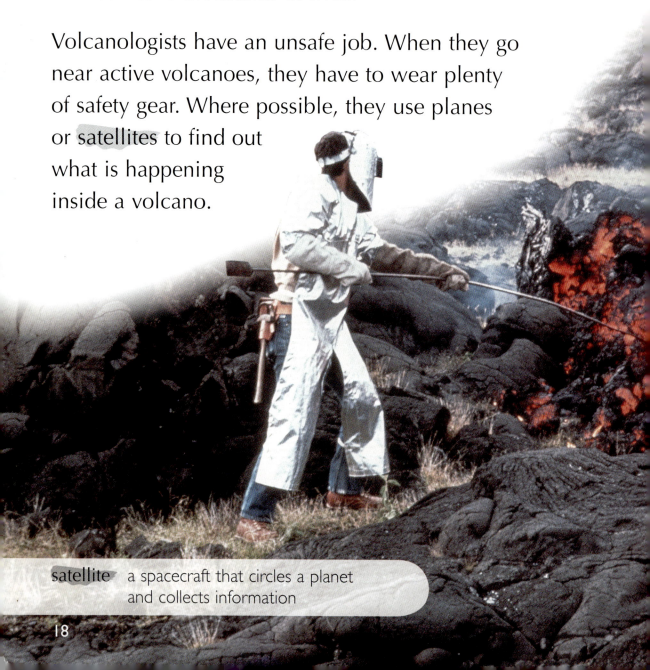

satellite   a spacecraft that circles a planet and collects information

Working on a Volcano

The word *volcano* comes from *Vulcan*, which is the name of the ancient Roman god of fire.

Volcanologists use long, metal sticks to collect lava. This lava soon cools into hard rock.

Special metal machines tell them how hot the lava is. These machines can read very high temperatures.

This machine is placed near the crater to record how much the volcano makes the ground shake.

Volcanologists wear helmets and silver suits to keep out the heat. They stay as far away from the hot lava as they can.

temperature   how hot or cold something is

19

Geysers and Hot Pools

In areas where volcanoes once existed,
there is often hot magma under the ground.
When rainwater sinks into the ground, the
magma heats it up.

Sometimes this hot water comes back to the
surface. Hot water that bubbles at ground level
forms hot pools. Fountains of boiling water that
shoot high into the air are called *geysers*.

Iceland is a cold country,
but people enjoy swimming
in its many hot springs.

Volcanic steam is used to make electricity in countries such as New Zealand and Iceland.

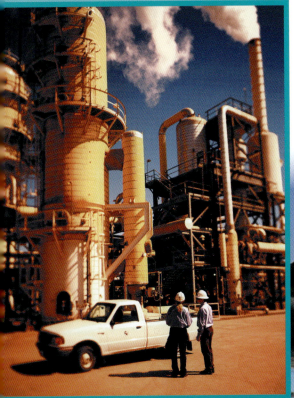

Hot Spots to Visit

Visitors to Rotorua, New Zealand, can see boiling mud pools. The pools smell like rotten eggs because of the gas that rises from them. Mud pools form when hot spring water mixes with rocks and soil.

Old Faithful is a geyser in Wyoming. Once or twice an hour, it spurts boiling water more than 100 feet into the air.

After a Volcano

Lava, ash, and rock can destroy the land for miles around a volcano. People and animals need to move away to avoid being harmed. Slowly, however, plants begin to grow, and life returns.

Some areas that are farther away from a volcano get only a thin layer of ash. The ash is full of nutrients that help crops grow.

Farmers in Costa Rica grow many crops, such as onions and corn, in the rich, volcanic soil.

nutrients   things that keep plants and animals healthy

These plants are growing on an old volcano. Over time, weather and plant roots will break up the rock. It then mixes with dead plants to form soil.

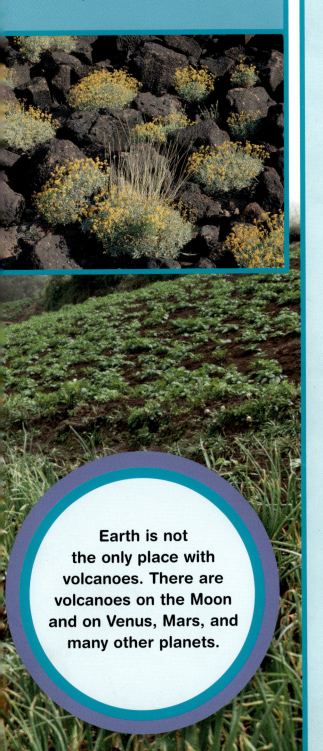

Earth is not the only place with volcanoes. There are volcanoes on the Moon and on Venus, Mars, and many other planets.

Activity Zone!

1. On a tray, make a model mountain out of modeling clay. Scoop out a hole in the top. Place a plastic cap from a spray bottle in the hole.

2. Pour $\frac{1}{4}$ cup of warm water into the cap. Stir in 1 tablespoon of baking soda and a few drops of red food coloring. Then quickly pour in $\frac{1}{4}$ cup of vinegar and stand back!

23

Find Out More!

1. What volcanoes are erupting now? Where are they? What are their names?

2. Where are the nearest volcanoes to you? What interesting facts can you find out about them?

To find out more about the ideas in *Fire and Ash*, visit **www.researchit.org** on the web.

Index